LAMBORGHINI

THE FASTEST

by
SHIRLEY HAINES
and
HARRY HAINES

THE ROURKE CORPORATION, INC.
Vero Beach, FL 32964

ACKNOWLEDGMENTS

The authors and publisher wish to thank AUTOMOBILI LAMBORGHINI, S.p.A., for invaluable assistance in compiling the photographs and technical information for this book. Special thanks are due Dominic Pecchia and Sandro Munari for locating the photographs listed below from Lamborghini. Ingrid Pussich provided the production information. And, more than to any other single person, appreciation is owed to Jim Kaminski, President of the Lamborghini Owners Club, for his continuous help, guidance, and encouragement.

Gratitude is expressed to the following Lamborghini owners who allowed their cars to be photographed and included in this book: Jon Pollock for the '65 350GT on page 5, and 8; Dieter Balogh for the '86 Quatro Valvole Countach on page 5; Scott Purodi for the '68 P400S Miura on pages 10-11; Beverly Overhauser for the '68 Islero on pages 14-15; and Jim Heady for the Silhouette on page 17.

Thanks to Ken Parker for the drawing of Italy on page 67.

PHOTO CREDITS:

Lamborghini: Diablos on the cover and on pages 4, 25, 26, and 27; 400GT on page 9; Espadas on page 12; Jarama on page 15; Jalpa on page 17; front facing Silhouette on page 17; red LM002 on page 18; Countach LP500 on page 20; and Countach by water on page 22.

Harry Haines: Jay Leno and 350GT on page 4; Countach and 350GT on page 5; St. Agata on page 6; 350GT on page 8; Miuras on pages 10-11; row of Espadas on page 13; Isleros on pages 14-15; Urraco on page 16; back facing Silhouette on page 17; marine engine and black LM002 on page 19; Countach backing and Countach with doors-up on page 21, Countaches at factory on page 23; and production line photos of Diablo on page 25.

Jim Kaminski: Ferruccio Lamborghini and tractor on page 7.

Library of Congress Cataloging-in-Publication Data

Haines, Shirley, 1935-
    Lamborghini: the fastest / by Shirley and Harry Haines.
      p. cm. – (Car classics)
    Includes index.
    Summary: Gives a brief history of the Lamborghini automobile describing some of its special features and some classic models.
    ISBN 0-86593-145-3
    1. Lamborghini automobile – Juvenile literature. [1. Lamborghini automobile.]
I. Haines, Harry, 1932- . II. Title. III. Series: Car classics (Vero Beach, Fla.)
TL215.L33H35 1991
629.222'2–dc20
                                                       91-7644
                                                            CIP
                                                            AC

CONTENTS

CHAPTER 1

THE LEGEND: FAST CARS

A 1990 Lamborghini Diablo. Reported by the press as the "fastest production road car in the world," it is the major car produced by the company.

Lamborghini cars are fascinating for everyone and are guaranteed to attract a crowd. Jay Leno of the NBC Tonight Show spent time looking at a newly restored 1965 350GT at a Lamborghini rally in Monterey, California in August, 1990.

All the world wants to know how fast a car will go. The faster the car, the greater the interest people seem to have in knowing its exact speed. Ultra-high performance automobiles, sometimes called exotic cars, are the result of this basic and widespread human interest.

For most of the years since the company was founded in 1964, Lamborghini has been making the fastest production road cars in the world. Lamborghini seems to be doing well in the exotic car business. In fact, many experts have referred to these cars as the best, the most exotic of the exotics. Car prices certainly support this belief. Model for model, year after year, Lamborghinis bring top dollar. In 1990, a new Diablo listed for $220,000 in the United States, and the company reports that all the cars are sold for two years in advance. The resale value of older Lamborghinis has climbed steadily since the 1980s and is frequently reported in car magazines.

Lamborghini cars are fast, innovative, beautiful, and famous. These legendary automobiles have only existed since 1963 and are the product of an amazing little company in St. Agata, Italy.

A 350GT and a Countach, roughly the earliest and the latest of the cars made by Lamborghini at the time this picture was taken. Production of the 350GT began in 1964, and the last Countach was made in July, 1990.

CHAPTER 2

FERRUCCIO LAMBORGHINI

Ferruccio (fair-ROOCH-ee-oh) Lamborghini is the man responsible for the car that bears his name. He was born April 28, 1916 in the small village of Renazzo, about 15 miles north of Bologna, Italy. The Lamborghinis were peasant farmers, and young Ferruccio spent his early years on the family farm.

When World War II came, Lamborghini was drafted into the Italian Army to work as a mechanic in a motor pool in Turkey. After the war he returned to the family farm near Bologna, and found a critical shortage of tractors. In response to this need, he began to assemble homemade tractors from leftover war vehicles. He prospered and soon built a factory near Bologna where he manufactured outstanding diesel tractors of his own design. By the mid-1950s the Lamborghini Tractor Company was one of Italy's largest farm machinery manufacturers. In 1960 he founded another plant to make home and commercial heating and air conditioning equipment.

Twice a millionaire by 1962, Ferruccio Lamborghini decided to go into the automobile business. Not surprisingly, he followed the same

Ferruccio Lamborghini (right) with visitor Jim Kaminski, president of the American Lamborghini Owners Club. This photo was taken at the Lamborghini farm in Panicarola, Italy, September 15, 1988 when Lamborghini was age 72.

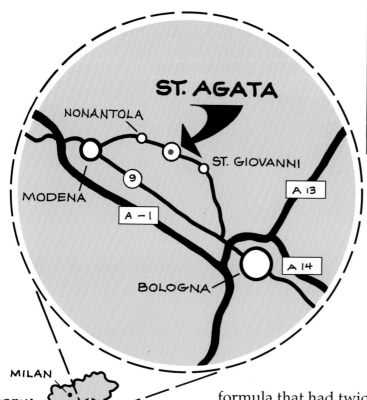

The tiny village of St. Agata is so small it is not listed on most maps.

The Lamborgini factory is located in St. Agata, Italy. The village is about 15 miles from Bologna and Modena.

formula that had twice before proved successful. He bought land in a small village, built a modern building, and filled it with state-of-the-art equipment. Then he hired the best talent he could find to design and build the ultra-high performance cars that would bear his name.

Automobili Lamborgini, S.p.A., as the company is now officially known, was launched with brilliant optimism but has had its ups and downs. It has always been a small operation making only about 400 cars per year. In 1972, Ferruccio Lamborghini grew tired of the financial problems and sold the company to Swiss investors. In 1979 it was declared legally bankrupt and turned over to an Italian court. The company was put back on its feet by the Mimran family, and they in turn sold to Detroit's Chrysler Corporation in 1987. Under Chrysler's new leadership, the company brought out the Diablo in 1990.

This small company that produces only 1.8 cars a day in the tiny village of St. Agata, Italy has once again regained the lead in world-class exotic cars. Its future looks bright for the 1990s.

CHAPTER 3

THE FIRST LAMBORGHINIS: 350GT AND 400GT

Lamborghini's first production car was the 350GT. A roomy two-seater, it created an overall graceful appearance. But while big and beautiful were important, the key to the success of the car – and the future of the new company – was the engine.

The Lamborghini V-12 was designed by one of the most famous names in automobile history, Giotto Bizzarrini. History records that the first Lamborghini V-12 roared to life on May 15, 1963 at the company's new factory in St. Agata, Italy. At 8000 rpm it showed an output of 360 horsepower on the European standard DIN scale, about 374 horsepower in today's SAE net measure. The 12 cylinders were set at a 60-degree angle. There were two valves per cylinder, and total displacement was 3464.5 cc.

Lamborghini's first production car, the 350GT. Body was by Touring. Big, beautiful and powerful, it had a 3.5 liter V-12 designed by Bizzarrini. Performance numbers are hard to find, but it was probably a 150-mph automobile.

Like Ferrari, Maserati, and other Italian sports car makers of the day, bodywork was done by a coach builder. Lamborghini chose a famous company, Carrozzeria Touring, to design and build the bodies for his new cars. Contracting a coach builder to build the bodies is a practice still followed by the company today.

The 400GT was remarkably similar to the 350GT. Many experts consider the 400 series the finest cars made by Lamborghini. The change in model name referred to the V-12; it grew to almost 4.0 liters, 320 hp.

The 400GT (and 400GT 2+2) looked much the same as the 350GT. The most prominent difference was in the headlights. The 400 series replaced each single, oval headlight with a pair of round ones. Production of the 350GT totaled 120 cars during the years 1964-1966. Only 23 400GT models were made in 1966. In mid-year it was changed to the 400GT 2+2, and an additional 250 cars were made through 1968. Production details on all Lamborghinis are given on pages 28-29.

CHAPTER 4

170 MPH: THE MIURA

Lamborghini became a world-class sports car manufacturer in 1966 with the introduction of a sensational new mid-engine car, the Miura (Me-YOUR-ah). Named for a Spanish fighting bull, it was the most exotic road car of the day. The Miura overshadowed every production-line Ferrari. At 170-plus mph, it was also the fastest road car ever made up to that time. And it was strikingly beautiful.

As the first mid-engine high performance road car, the Miura was the front runner of the late 1960s. But the all-new design was mechanically troublesome, hot, noisy, uncomfortable to ride in, and a handful to drive. The company made two formal redesigns and then stopped production in 1972.

Miura was the car that had everything: beautiful proportions, new technology, and the fastest speedometer numbers. Premiered at the 1966 Geneva Auto Show, it created a sensation.

To examine the engine, it was necessary to open both doors and pull a T-handle behind each seat. Roughly the back third of the body swung up and down. The unusual headlight design was later copied by Porsche for their 928 series. Total Miura production added up to only 764 cars between 1966 and 1972.

Bob Wallace, the test driver for the early Lamborghini cars, described the Miura this way: "It was a milestone car in what a GT car should be." With beautiful design, new technology, and unmatched speed, Lamborghini in the late 1960s was the hottest car on the road and the new leader of exotic cars.

CHAPTER 5

THE BIG SELLER: THE ESPADA

Two views of Lamborghini's most popular car of the 60s and 70s, the Espada. The name Espada is Spanish for the sword used by bullfighters. In its day, it was the fastest four-place car on the road.

From 1968 to 1978, 1,220 Lamborghini Espadas (s-PAH-dahs) were produced. While this may not seem like a large number of cars, it was almost double the figure of any other model until the Countach.

The success of the Espada was probably due to three main factors. First of all, it was a large roomy car with seating for four passengers. Then, too, its body design was generally regarded as one of the most beautiful cars of its day. Finally, the now-famous 4000 cc Lamborghini V-12 engine made the Espada one of the fastest cars on the road.

During this time period, the company was trying to make three basic cars: a top-of-the-line hot rod (the Miura, later the Countach), a two-place gentleman's coupé (the Islero, later the Jarama), and a big roomy four-place car, the Espada. Many people wanted the Espada, and it became the biggest seller for 10 years.

Several experts described the Espada as a "blend of contrasts." It was a sedan on the inside and a sports car on the outside. Although it looked large, at 186.5 inches, it was about the same length as the U.S. compacts of the late 1960s. With its 3.9 liter V-12 mounted in front, the Espada was the fastest four-seater on the market and one of the fastest automobiles in the world. Top speed was said to be 155 mph.

Espadas lined up at the Lamborghini Concours in Monterey, California on August 17, 1990. The Espada usually outnumbers all other models (except sometimes the Countach) at this and other car shows.

CHAPTER 6

1968 TO 1978: ISLERO AND JARAMA

When the 400GT was discontinued in 1968, the Islero (eez-LAIR-oh) was introduced as its replacement. The new car used the same chassis and engine but came with an all-new body. Its most prominent styling feature was covered headlights.

The Islero offered impressive numbers. Lamborghini increased the V-12 compression to 10.8:1 and reported a top speed of 161 mph at 7800 rpm. *Sports Car World* wrote that the Islero would do 0 – 60 in 6.2 seconds and set the top speed at 160 mph going "flat-out" at 7500 rpm.

If the Islero had been the only Lamborghini in 1968 and 1969, it probably would have been a winner. But it was sandwiched in between the hotshot Miura and the big four-place Espada and, by comparison, came off third best. Only 225 were made, and the last one left St. Agata in April, 1970.

The Jarama (J is pronounced as Y in Italian, "yah-RAH-mah") was introduced as successor to the Islero. No one knew it at the time, but it was to be the last of the front-engine cars from Lamborghini. Marcello Gandini, the man who designed the Espada and the Miura, was commissioned to do the new car. One of the most interesting aspects of the Jarama's appearance was the half-covered headlights.

A beautifully maintained 1968 Islero. It is reported that Ferruccio Lamborghini himself was the dominant influence in determining the design of this car. He wanted a big, roomy, fast "businessman's" car, which the Islero definitely is!

The Jarama, with its half-covered headlights, was the last front-engine car made by Lamborghini.

The Jarama had the misfortune to come along at a time when the company was having financial troubles. For this and other reasons, only 327 Jaramas were made. The last one rolled off the line in 1978.

CHAPTER 7

LAMBORGHINI V-8S: URRACO, SILHOUETTE, JALPA

A Urraco at the factory in St. Agata. The Urraco was initially marketed as a 2+2 model.

In its entire history, Lamborghini so far has made only three cars that did *not* use V-12 engines based upon the original Bizzarrini. They were the Urraco (you-RAH-koh), Silhouette, and Jalpa (YAHL-pa). All three were powered by the same basic engine, a 90-degree V-8 that started at 2462 cc and gradually grew to 3.5 liters.

The Urraco was introduced in 1972 and called a 2+2. The back seats, however, were a joke since even the smallest of human bodies could not be accommodated. Many other parts of the car were disappointing, too, and production was halted in 1979 after 780 had been built.

The Silhouette appeared in 1976. Several improvements were immediately obvious. First, it was an honest two-seater, with no pretense about trying to squeeze midgets into the back seats. It also offered a first for Lamborghini, a removable targa top. Overall, though, the Silhouette was too much like the Urraco, and the resulting poor sales forced a halt. Production ended in 1979 after only three years and a total of 52 cars.

Two different Silhouettes. The front facing photo was taken at the factory, and the rear shot of a rare California car was taken at the Monterey Concours.

Hoping the third time would bring success, the company introduced yet another V-8 in 1982, the Jalpa. Promoted as "the Countach's little brother," the new car did have a number of design similarities. People unfamiliar with Lamborghinis could confuse a Jalpa with the bigger car. But without the big V-12 engine, Jalpa sales could never seem to rise above the red ink. Customers who paid for a Lamborghini wanted a V-12. The last Jalpa, number 410, left the factory in 1988.

When the first V-8 was on the drawing board in the early 1970s, Lamborghini looked at the big market enjoyed by Porsche's 911 and Ferrari's Dino 246GT. The St. Agata company's goal was to produce and sell 1,000 V-8 powered cars per year. In the entire time period between 1972 and 1988, about 16 years, only 1,242 cars were made with V-8 engines.

The Jalpa, Lamborghini's final entry into the V-8 market. Production for this model ended in 1988.

CHAPTER 8

OFF-ROAD AND BOATS:
LM002 AND MARINE ENGINES

Above: A marine version of the classic Lamborghini V-12. This engine is rated at 880 hp at 6650 rpm and will be installed in a racing boat.

Left: The LM002, off-road and climbing. Autocar *magazine noted that it could "take steep hills at an angle of 70 degrees without falling over."*

Besides its sports cars, Automobili Lamborghini has become involved in a couple of other related areas. The first is the LM002, a high-quality off-road vehicle unlike any other.

If a person is looking for a four-wheel drive, super off-roader, with V-12 engine, the LM002 would seem to be in a class by itself. Brock Yates, writing in *Car and Driver*, referred to it as "Rambo Lambo" and called his experience driving the LM002 "the closest thing to a street-legal Tiger Tank known to man."

"Four years from the start of production, the Lamborghini LM002 is still a unique car with its own share of the market for high-performance all-terrain vehicles." This quote, perhaps the classic understatement of all time, is from the company's report to shareholders dated December, 1989. At that time, a total of 200 LM002s had been made. The company expects to end production in 1991 after 300 of these vehicles have been sold.

Marine engines have also been a highly successful market for Lamborghini. Starting in 1983 with an adaptation of the legendary 60 degree V-12, the first engines were produced for racing craft. They had 8000 cc, compression ratio 9.2:1, and power of 670 hp at 6200 rpm. Increases over the years have boosted this powerful engine to 880 hp at 6650 rpm. In 1989 alone, Lamborghini-powered boats won 13 of the most famous international races.

Right: Another LM002 parked at the factory in St. Agata. Top speed is reported at 125 mph and 0 – 62.5 in 8.5 seconds.

CHAPTER 9

LAMBORGHINI SCORES BIG: COUNTACH

A Countach LP500. This model was made between 1982 and 1985 with an enlarged 5.0 liter engine. The factory claimed 440 DIN horsepower at 7400 rpm and a top speed of 185 mph.

"If the Miura made Lamborghini's name famous, the Countach (COON-tahtsch) made it immortal," said Pete Lyons in his outstanding book, *The Complete Lamborghini.*

Just as Ferrari has joined with one principal designer, Pininfarina, Lamborghini's most successful body designs are the creations of a single person, Marcello Gandini. His most impressive car has been the Lamborghini Countach. Considered a major breakthrough in automotive design, the Countach has probably been the most acclaimed car of the 1970s and 1980s. It couldn't have come at a better time for a company troubled by financial losses, multiple changes in leadership and ownership, and eventual bankruptcy. It is not too much to say that Countach is the car that saved Lamborghini.

Doors that swing up to open have been a Countach trademark. A surprise design feature, also standard for 18 years, has been the headlight placement. Twin lights pop up behind the white covers for parking lights.

The technical excellence of the car was primarily the work of Paolo Stanzani who was, at the time, the chief engineer at Lamborghini. It was his decision to remount the now-proven V-12. He installed the engine lengthways in the back (posterior) and named it the LP400. The new car created a sensation when introduced at the Geneva Auto Show in 1971.

Top speed for the first Countach was probably in the mid-180s. Bob Wallace, the original factory test driver, reported 180.2 mph at 7600 rpm in the number 3 prototype on a timed 5-kilometer stretch of private superhighway at the Fiat automobile factory. Wallace thought he could have reached 7800 rpm and 186.4 mph (the magic 300 kilometers per hour) had conditions been right.

In the November, 1986, issue of *Automobile*, Mel Nichols stated that a Quattrovalvole model had run 0 – 60 mph in 5 seconds and the quarter-mile in exactly 13 seconds. This was done at Italy's high-speed Nardo test track under ideal conditions.

How do you back up in a Countach? Open the door, slide over and sit on the door sill. This photograph demonstrates the technique made necessary by poor rear visibility.

CHAPTER 10

25TH ANNIVERSARY: COUNTACH ENDS

Production for the Countach ran 18 years. Starting in 1972, the last 15 cars came off the line in July, 1990. Five different models were made, and a total of 1,972 cars were produced during this time.

The Italian word *countach* is difficult to translate exactly into English. It is a slang expression that means something like, "Good Lord!" It is the sort of thing a young Italian male might utter to express appreciation for a particularly attractive female.

A "25th Anniversary" model Countach. This was the last of the 5 models produced from 1972 to 1990. The most distinctive external change was the addition of air scoops in front of the wheels.

A historic photo taken at the factory in late July, 1990. These are the last 15 Countaches produced, the end of an 18-year era.

The fifth and final version of the Countach was introduced in 1988. Called the "25th Anniversary," it was so named to recognize the 25th year since the founding of the company in 1963.

The 25th Anniversary model represented the Countach at its peak. Approximately 650 cars were made during the three-year run from 1988 to 1990. Company figures reported the V-12 at 5167 cc producing 455 hp at 7000 rpm. Top speed was 184 mph, and acceleration from 0 – 62.5 mph was 5 seconds flat.

The back end of the most famous sports car ever made. A small "25," circled by a wreath on the left side identifies the car as a "25th Anniversary" model.

CHAPTER 11

BIG NEWS FOR THE 1990S: THE DIABLO

Creating legends is not easy. Lamborghini has already done it twice with the Miura in 1966 and the Countach in 1972. More than a few automobile enthusiasts have been wondering about the new car for the 1990s.

Developing a worthy successor to the Countach presents great risks for the company. It is exactly like the situation Porsche found itself in during the 1960s. Porsche's 356 was produced from 1948 to 1965, 18 years. When the new Porsche 911 was introduced in 1965, the future of the company was literally riding on public acceptance of the new car. So it is now with Lamborghini. The new Diablo must be better than the supercar it replaces. And one of the biggest problems is that the word "better" is not clearly defined.

Diablo seems to be meeting the challenge beautifully. The car is beautiful and mixes new features with those found on the Countach. The 60-degree V-12, a hallmark of Lamborghini's success over the years, is the same basic engine, even though it has been refined for more power. The engine is now 5.7 liters, 4 valves per cylinder and 4 camshafts, compression ratio 10.0:1, power rated at 492 hp at 7000 rpm. Such impressive numbers, combined with a 27-year history of proven excellence should earn the engine a top rating among world-class sports cars.

Technology is an important factor. People who pay huge sums of money for an exotic car want innovation. The Diablo's biggest innovation is optional 4-wheel drive. All-wheel drive in a car that tops 200 mph sounds incredible. Lamborghini calls it VT (for viscous traction) and plans to release it in the 1991 models.

Diablo prototype. This picture was probably taken in January, 1990 in St. Agata. Note the characteristic side windows that slant down.

St. Agata was an exciting place to be in 1990. These photos were taken during July of that year and show the first Diablos coming off the production line.

CHAPTER 12

WORLD'S FASTEST ROAD CAR: THE DIABLO

How fast can the Diablo go? Lamborghini reports that its top speed is 202.1 mph with acceleration from 0 to 100 kilometers (62.5 mph) in 4.09 seconds. When the Diablo was introduced in 1990, these were the fastest numbers of any production road car in the world.

But speed isn't everything. A Ferrari F40 reports a top speed of 201 mph. If a car is fast, really fast, then other factors become equally if not more important.

The Diablo was designed by Marcello Gandini, the same genius who created the Miura and the Countach. This time, Lamborghini placed more emphasis on aerodynamics. A major limitation of the Countach was its high Cd (coefficient of drag). The car looked fast, but wind tunnel tests rated it similar to a barn door. The Cd for the Diablo is reported to be among the best in its class.

Above and above right: Front and rear views of the Diablo prototype. These pictures were made in early 1990 at the factory in St. Agata. Once again, as has happened many times since 1964, a Lamborghini is reported to be the fastest production road car in the world.

The latest refinement of the famous Lamborghini V-12. The Diablo's engine is reported at 5.7 liters and rated 492 hp at 7000 rpm.

Another major improvement in the new car are the doors and windows. Diablo windows, distinctively different, open down completely into the doors. Side visibility is outstanding because of the belt-line dip of the new windows. The doors, still opening vertically as on the Countach, now have a lower door sill for easier passenger entry. The interior, as expected, is elegant and refined.

The more years a car is in production, the harder it is to replace. In other words, because the Countach enjoyed 19 years of production, the Diablo's challenge to replace it is especially big. Is Diablo meeting that challenge? Yes, and with flying colors!

The new technology at Lamborghini will include an option of 4-wheel drive for a 200-plus mph car.

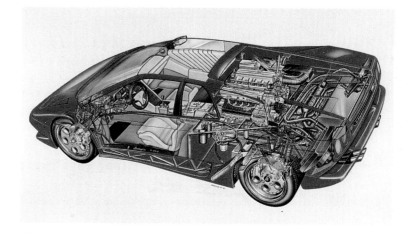

CHAPTER 13

LAMBORGHINI OVER THE YEARS

	Model	Engine	Engine capacity	Body	Designer	Production from - up to	Units produced
	350 GT		3500	Berlinetta 2 Posti	Touring	1964-1966	120
	400 GT 2+2	L401	3927	Berlinetta 2 Posti	Touring	1966-1966	23
	400 GT 2+2 /1	L401	3927	Coupé 2+2	Touring	1966-1968	250
	ISLERO	L401	3927	Coupé 2+2	Marazzi	1968-1968	125
	ISLERO S	L401	3927	Coupé 2+2	Marazzi	1969-1969	100
	MIURA	P400	3929	Berlinetta 2 Posti	Bertone	1966-1969	474
	MIURA S	P400	3929	Berlinetta 2 Posti	Bertone	1969-1971	140
	MIURA SV	P400	3929	Berlinetta 2 Posti	Bertone	1971-1972	150
	ESPADA	L401	3929	Coupé 4 Posti	Bertone	1968-1978	1220
	JARAMA	L401	3929	Coupé 2+2	Bertone	1970-1973	177
	JARAMA S	L401	3929	Coupé 2+2	Bertone	1973-1978	150

Model	Engine	Engine capacity	Body	Designer	Production from - up to	Units produced	
URRACO P 250	L240	2463	Coupé 2+2	Bertone	1972-1976	520	
URRACO P 200	L200	1973	Coupé 2+2	Bertone	1975-1977	66	
URRACO P 300	L302	2996	Coupé 2+2	Bertone	1975-1979	194	
SILHOUETTE	L302	2996	Targa 2+2	Bertone	1976-1979	52	
COUNTACH LP 400	L406	3929	Coupé 2 Posti	Bertone	1972-1978	150	
COUNTACH S	L406	3929	Coupé 2 Posti	Bertone	1978-1982	235	
COUNTACH LP 500	L503	4754	Coupé 2 Posti	Bertone	1982-1985	323	
COUNTACH 4 valv.	L50/V4	5167	Coupé 2 Posti	Bertone	1985-1988	610	
JALPA	L353	3485	Targa 2 Posti	Bertone	1982-1988	410	
COUNTACH 25°	L50/V4	5167	Coupé 2 Posti	Bertone	1988-1990	653	
LM 002	L510	5167	4WD 4 Posti	Lamborghini	1986-1991	300	
DIABLO	L510	5700	Coupé 2 Posti	Gandini	1990-?		

CHAPTER 14

LAMBORGHINI: IMPORTANT DATES

1916 Ferruccio Lamborghini is born in a small village just north of Bologna, Italy.

1962 Lamborghini buys land in the village of St. Agata, Italy and begins to build the factory.

1963 The first Lamborghini V-12, designed and built by Giotto Bizzarrini, is tested in the new factory. At 8000 rpm it shows 360 hp; total displacement is 3.5 liters.

1963 The first car is called a GTV.

1964 The first production cars are made. Called the 350GT, they are big, beautiful, and fast. Body is made by Touring.

1966 The 400GT and later the 400GT 2+2 are introduced.

1966 Miura creates a sensation at the Geneva Auto Show. At over 170 mph, it is the fastest production road car of its day.

1968 The 400GT is discontinued and the Islero introduced as its replacement.

1968 The Espada is introduced and is the fastest four-place car on the road.

1970 The Jarama is introduced as a replacement for the Islero.

1971 The Countach prototype is shown at the Geneva Auto Show.

1972 The new V-8 powered Urraco is introduced.

1972 Countach production begins with the LP400, and Miura is phased out.

1972 Ferruccio Lamborghini sells the company, Automobili Ferruccio Lamborghini, S.p.A., to Swiss investors.

1976 Silhouette is introduced. V-8 powered, it is the first Lamborghini with an open top.

1978 Automobili Ferruccio Lamborghini, S.p.A. declares bankruptcy.

1979 Production ends for Urraco and Silhouette.

1981 Mimran family assumes control, forms Nuova Automobili Ferruccio Lamborghini, S.p.A.

1982 Countach is upgraded to LP500, a larger engine. Jalpa is introduced.

1985 Countach Quattrovalvole is introduced. Plans begin for Diablo.

1986 The LM002 is introduced.

1987 Lamborghini S.p.A. is purchased by Chrysler Corporation. Company renamed Automobili Lamborghini, S.p.A.

1988 A new and final model of the Countach, the 25th Anniversary, is introduced. Production is cancelled for the Jalpa.

1990 Diablo production begins.

1991 LM002 production ends.

GLOSSARY

cc – Cubic centimeters. Refers to the amount of space in the engine cylinders. The larger the number of ccs the larger the engine and power. One hundreth of a liter.

DIN – Deutsches Institute fuer Normung. The acronym used for many years to indicate a standard way of calculating the horsepower of an automobile.

dohc – Dual overhead cam. Refers to two drives (instead of one) that operate the levers or cams which open and close the valves and are located over the head of the engine.

km/h – Kilometers per hour. The speed of a car in kilometers.

mph – Miles per hour. The speed of a car in miles.

SAE – Society of Automotive Engineers. The acronym most often used today to indicate a standard way of calculating the horsepower of an automobile.

targa – A car with a removable top. Unlike a convertible, which is topless from the windshield back, the targa usually has some kind of passenger protection both in front of and behind the passenger seats.

Countach (COON-tahtsch) – An Italian slang expression, something close to "Good Lord!"

Diablo (dee-AH-blow) – The name of a famous bull in Spain.

Espada (s-PAH-dah) – The sword used by bull fighters.

Islero (eez-LAIR-oh) – The bull that killed famed matador Manuel Rodriguez in a famous bullfight in 1947.

Jalpa (YAHL-pa) – A breed of bull found in Spain.

Jarama (yah-RAHM-ah) – The district in Spain that is noted for breeding fighting bulls and the race track outside Madrid that often hosted the Gran Prix.

Miura (me-YOUR-ah) – A Spanish fighting bull.

Urraco (you-RAH-koh) – A young bull.

INDEX